**READING AND WRITING WORKSHOPS EDITION**

# NATIONAL GEOGRAPHIC Explorer!

## CONTENTS

# Sneakers

## THE ALL★STARS OF FOOTWEAR

**Happy Feet.**
Sneakers make your feet feel good. They're lighter, softer, and more cushiony than leather-soled shoes. Maybe that's why sneakers are America's most popular shoe.

JOSEPH

L ook down at your feet. What are you wearing on them? Odds are the answer is **sneakers**. Sneakers are everywhere. But how much do you know about this popular footwear? How were sneakers invented? What are they made of? And why are they called "sneakers" anyway?

## Rooted in Rubber

The story of sneakers started about 500 years ago. That's when European explorers in Central and South America noticed Native Americans playing with an unusual ball. The ball was made from a milky, white liquid that oozed out of the *cahuchu* (ka OO choo) tree. The liquid, known today as **latex** (LAY tex), hardened as it dried.

Native Americans had practical uses for latex too. They spread the sticky liquid on their feet. Once it dried, it formed a very thin "shoe" that protected their feet from water. They also made waterproof bottles with latex.

When explorers brought latex samples back to Europe in the early 1700s, scientists started searching for their own ways to use it. In 1770, an English chemist named Joseph Priestley discovered that the gummy stuff could rub out pencil marks. People dubbed it "rubber," and the name stuck.

## The Right Stuff

By the early 1800s, manufacturers in the United States and Europe had found many uses for rubber. They used the stretchy, waterproof stuff for raincoats, hoses, elastic bands, and more. But rubber wasn't very good for making most things. It got too brittle in the cold and too sticky in the heat.

That changed in 1839. An inventor named Charles Goodyear mixed rubber and a smelly yellow chemical called sulfur. Then he accidentally spilled it onto a hot stove. The resulting glop stayed firm and stretchy whatever the temperature. It was called **vulcanized** (VUL can ized) **rubber**, named after Vulcan, the Roman god of fire.

## Sneaking Around

A few years later, manufacturers teamed vulcanized rubber soles, or shoe bottoms, with a tough fabric called **canvas**. The result was comfortable, lightweight shoes. Up until then, almost everyone wore leather shoes with hard soles that clomped loudly with each step. The new rubber-soled shoes were very quiet. You could easily sneak around in them, so people started calling them "sneakers."

At first, sneakers weren't very popular. For one thing, they were expensive. And people were more excited about using vulcanized rubber to make tires for bicycles—and, later, cars. But in 1916, a rubber company introduced a simple sneaker called Keds. Its price was low, so many people could afford a pair. Keds were a huge success.

A year later, another company called Converse created the first basketball sneaker. The All-Star model featured rubber soles that kept players from slipping on the court. They also had canvas tops that went up around the ankle for good support. Sneakers were off and running.

JACK HORNADY

# Great Leaps
## in Sneaker Design

Sneakers are always on the move. Check out these giant steps in sneaker history.

This tough rubber sole the first aff

◀ **Getting a Grip.**
The rubber soles on sneakers give athletes like Serena Williams good traction.

**1917**

**Canvas High-Tops**
Extending the canvas top to the ankle gave the shoe wearer more support.

**1970s**

**Waffle Sole**
This lighter, notched sole helped athletes run faster.

**1990s**

**Laceless Upper**
High-tech elastic webbing around the top of the foot replaced laces.

ed with
oppers
eakers.

**Run 'n Roll.**
Sometimes you're on the run. Sometimes you're on a roll. Now there are sneakers that serve both needs. Some have wheels that pop out with the turn of a switch or a key. Others, like these, have removable wheels.

COURTESY OF HEELYS

# Gaining Speed

During World War II, the United States' supply of natural rubber was cut off. So scientists figured out how to use chemicals to make **synthetic** (sin THEH tick), or human-made, rubber. We still use both types of rubber today.

After the war, Americans had more leisure time for sports. A sneaker boom began. In the 1950s, schools required students to wear sneakers for gym classes and dances so they wouldn't scuff gymnasium floors. For that reason, people started calling sneakers "gym shoes."

# Stepping Up Design

It wasn't until the fitness craze of the 1970s that many people started taking sneakers seriously, though.

Track coach Bill Bowerman was one of these people. He realized that if he could create lighter sneakers, his runners would save energy. In fact, shaving just one ounce off the shoes would help. The runner's legs would lift 200 fewer pounds over the course of a mile. That could help his athletes win races.

One day in 1971, inspired by his breakfast, Bowerman poured liquid rubber into his wife's waffle iron, and let it harden. The experiment ruined the waffle iron. But it resulted in the first "waffle soles." These were lighter than flat soles because of all the notches in the waffle pattern. Plus they gave better **traction**, or grip. A new model for sneaker soles hit the pavement.

By the end of the 1980s, shoe designers were getting quite creative with design improvements. Built-in air pumps offered extra foot support. Gel in the sole improved cushioning. And plastic springs in the heels absorbed even more of the impact, or force, from running and jumping. Sneakers were becoming high-tech.

## Wordwise

**canvas:** strong, woven fabric, often made of cotton

**latex:** milky substance some trees produce that hardens when exposed to air

**sneakers:** rubber-soled athletic shoes, usually with canvas or nylon tops

**synthetic:** human-made, not natural

**traction:** the "grip" of your shoes on the floor or ground

**vulcanized rubber:** rubber combined with sulfur over heat

## Modern Wonders

Today, sneakers are big business. In 2000, people in the United States spent more than $15 billion on them. That means they purchased more than 405 million pairs.

Modern sneaker designs jump far beyond the first canvas-and-rubber model. Some of the changes are kind of wacky. For example, in the early 1990s, sneakers got even lighter—but not in the sense of weight. Designers added lights that flashed in the shoe's heels with every step.

Recently, sneakers have picked up speed too. That's because some of them have pop-out wheels on the bottom. You can either walk along on the rubber soles or release the wheels and really get rolling.

Whether you wear sneakers to play sports or for fashion flair, the choices today are endless. So the next time you get a new pair of sneakers, take a good look at how they're made. Think about what goes into them and all the history behind them. Then slip them on and take off!

# DESIGN FEAT
## ★ FROM TOP TO BOTTOM ★

**UPPER**

**Laces**

**Tongue**

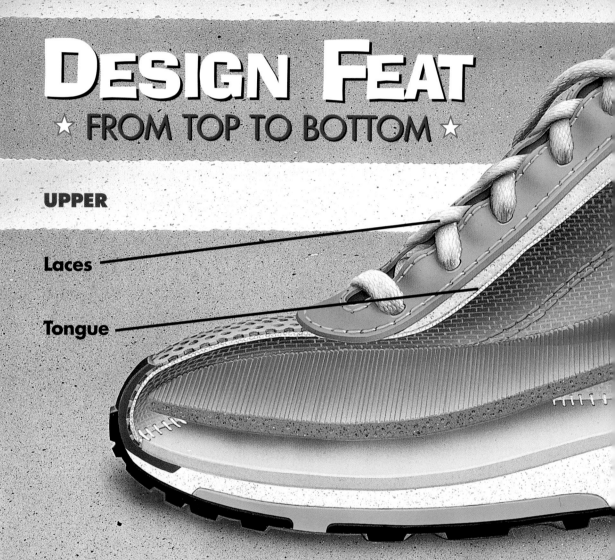

**T**he modern sneaker is an amazing creation. It's made up of many different parts. Yet all the pieces work together to keep your foot comfortable and help prevent injuries. A sneaker also adds a little spring to your step, so you can run and jump better.

**UPPER**
This is the top area of a sneaker. Its main job is to hold the sole against the bottom of your foot. Most uppers are made of canvas, leather, or nylon. With the midsole, the upper keeps your foot steady, so it doesn't turn and twist too much.

**Laces:** These secure the upper to your foot. They are usually made from shoestring, but velcro straps are also popular. Some modern sneakers don't have laces at all. You just slide your foot right in.

**Tongue:** The tongue keeps the laces from pressing down on your foot.

**SOLE**

**Insole**

**Midsole**

**Outsole**

**SOLE**
This is the bottom layer of a sneaker. Its main jobs are to hold the foot in place, provide cushioning, and keep the foot from slipping and sliding.

**Insole:** This thin foam insert fits inside your shoe. It provides some cushioning, but its main purpose is to keep your foot in place.

**Midsole:** This thick, springy, foam rubber section serves as a cushion for your foot.

To increase cushioning, some midsoles have special features like the red air pockets in the midsole above.

**Outsole:** This bottom layer of tough rubber grips the ground, giving you traction. (Think of traction as what you *don't* have when you slide across the kitchen floor in socks.) The pattern in the outsole determines how much traction the shoe has.

STEPHEN R. WAGNER

**Volcanoes are some of the hottest places on Earth. They are also some of the coolest.**

Hot Spots

*Kilauea, Hawaii*

G. BRAD LEWIS, GETTY IMAGES

## By Beth Geiger

Joanne Green carefully put her foot down as if it were her last step. It could have been. The hardened **lava** underfoot was blazing hot. A nearby river of glowing lava splashed melted rock.

"The heat on your face is very, very intense," said Green. "If you aren't careful," she went on, "you'll melt your boots on the hot rock. Or worse!"

Green, you see, is a **volcanologist.** She's a scientist who studies volcanoes. To learn about these superheated spots, she gets as close to them as she can.

## Towering Infernos

Green was studying Kilauea. It's a volcano in Hawaii. It's just one of nearly 600 volcanoes on Earth's land. Many more rise from the ocean floor. All together, there are 1,500 active volcanoes worldwide.

Active volcanoes, however, make up only a small fraction of all mountains of fire. Many others are dormant, or "sleeping." These volcanoes haven't erupted in a long time. Some may never erupt again. Then there are extinct volcanoes. They fizzled out thousands or even millions of years ago.

All kinds of volcanoes—active, dormant, or extinct—are important. Volcanoes made 80 percent of Earth's surface. Most of our fertile soils came from volcanoes. And much of the air we breathe was erupted by them.

## It's About the Lava

A volcano is an opening, or **vent,** into Earth's hot interior. Molten rock, or **magma,** rises through the vent. When the magma blasts onto Earth's surface, it's called lava.

Not all lava is the same. Some volcanoes make runny lava. It flows very fast, like pancake batter. Runny lava forms a gentle slope called a shield volcano.

Other volcanoes erupt thick, sticky lava. It flows slowly, like toothpaste. This kind of lava cannot flow very far. It forms a mountain with steep slopes. It's called a composite volcano.

Composite volcanoes can erupt violently. A blast can hurl ash and lava at more than 600 miles per hour. Sometimes an eruption blows away large chunks of the volcano itself. All that's left is a steaming **caldera.**

**Real Fireworks.** *Lava explodes as it hits the Pacific Ocean. The molten rock flowed downhill from Kilauea, a volcano in Hawaii.*

# The Ring of Fire

Three-quarters of all volcanoes rise near the rim of the Pacific Ocean. This circle of hot spots is called the Ring of Fire (see map).

It's no accident that so many volcanoes are located there. The Ring of Fire is an area where some of the plates that form Earth's surface meet.

Sometimes when plates meet, one of them moves under the other. The lower one melts, forming magma. This magma squeezes through cracks in the surrounding rock. The magma can then burst through Earth's surface to build a new volcano or erupt from an old one.

**Busy Place.** *TOP: Kilauea has been erupting since 1983. It's the most active volcano on Earth. ABOVE: Cooling lava forms rock. That's how the Hawaiian Islands developed.*

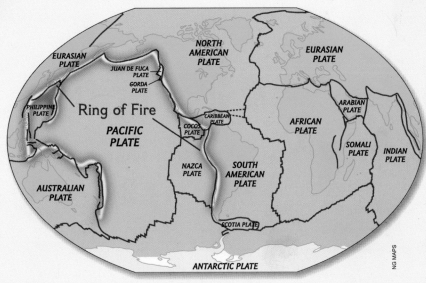

13

## Living With a Volcano

All active volcanoes affect the plants and animals that live around them. They make rich soils for plants to grow in. The plants attract all kinds of animals. Volcanoes even change the way people live. Farmers grow crops on rich volcanic soils. Tourists vacation near the beautiful mountains. Cities grow in the valleys beneath the peaks.

But life near an active volcano isn't easy. Sometimes the peaks turn into dangerous mountains of fire. When that happens, you don't want to be anywhere nearby.

## A Sleeping Giant Awakens

One of the most scenic U.S. volcanoes was Mount St. Helens. It's about 95 miles south of Seattle, Washington. The mighty mountain had last erupted in 1857.

Over the years, millions of people moved to the area around Mount St. Helens. Thousands more visited each year.

After all, the snowcapped volcano seemed peaceful and calm. But that all changed on the morning of May 18, 1980. At 8:32 a.m. a powerful earthquake rattled the area. Suddenly the north side of the volcano exploded.

**Blowing Its Top.** *An old photo shows visitors how Mount St. Helens looked before May 1980.*

14

## Changing Land

Hot ash and steam surged down the volcanic slopes at 200 miles per hour. When the smoke cleared, it looked like the top of the mountain had been chopped off. More than 1,000 feet was gone. A swath of land stretching 15 miles from the volcano was destroyed.

Today the volcano continues to erupt. But now it is slowly rebuilding itself. One day in the distant future, it will look much like it used to. But it is destined to repeat its violent past and destroy itself again.

## Wordwise

**caldera:** crater left from a violent eruption

**lava:** melted rock erupted from a volcano

**magma:** melted rock inside Earth

**vent:** hole or crack in Earth's surface

**volcanologist:** scientist who studies volcanoes

## Mount St. Helens Erupts

**Picture–Perfect?** *Mount St. Helens looked calm and peaceful on May 18, 1980.*
*It wasn't. Scientists knew something would happen. But no one knew exactly when.*

**Dark Day.** *The mountain exploded at 8:32 a.m. Ash soared 60,000 feet into the air. The blast produced 400 million tons of dust. It blanketed 230 square miles.*

# Inside a Volcano

An ash cloud forms above a volcano.

Earth's outermost layer is called the crust.

**M**ost people think that volcanoes are simply large mountains that erupt lava. But a volcano actually starts deep beneath Earth's surface, or crust.

The layer below the crust is called the mantle. It is very hot. The heat can melt rock. Sometimes pressure forces this heated rock through cracks in the crust. This can form a volcano.

Volcanoes form on all Earth's continents, even icy Antarctica. The mountains of fire also rise from the ocean floor.

Use the diagram to learn about the different parts of a volcano.

Lava is molten rock that flows from a volcano.

A crater is the opening at the top of a volcano.

Molten rock rises through the central vent.

Magma is molten rock inside a volcano.

A magma chamber lies deep inside a volcano.

ARTWORK BY PRECISION GRAPHICS

# Hawaii
## Island Chain

For many people, Hawaii is a lush, green paradise. But this chain of islands has a red-hot history. The islands are made of lava. They formed from underwater volcanoes in the Pacific Ocean.

## Hot Spot

The Hawaiian Islands sit near a superheated area of Earth's crust. Temperatures under the crust are so high there that they can actually melt rock. Scientists call this area the Hawaiian hot spot.

For millions of years, the Hawaiian hot spot has melted holes through the Pacific Plate. This plate is one of the largest in Earth's crust. It makes up the floor of the vast Pacific Ocean.

Like other plates, the Pacific Plate moves slowly. It travels about 10 centimeters a year. It slides directly over the Hawaiian hot spot.

## Volcanoes, Old and New

Five million years ago, the hot spot burned a hole through the Pacific Plate. Magma, or hot rock, spilled out onto the ocean floor. Over time, this rock piled up into a giant mound. At last, it jutted out of the ocean. The island of Kauai was born!

Kauai was the first Hawaiian Island to form. It wasn't the last. Over many years, the Pacific Plate carried Kauai past the hot spot.

But the hot spot kept burning. As the plate moved, it scorched new holes in the crust. New mounds grew from the ocean floor. Each mound formed another island.

Today, most of the islands have moved past the hot spot. Their volcanoes are now extinct. Only the island of Hawaii is still erupting. Someday, it too will grow quiet. Yet the hot spot will continue to burn— and to form new islands.

**Hot History.** *Kauai is the oldest of the Hawaiian Islands. This chain of islands formed over a hot spot on the ocean floor.*

# How the Islands Formed

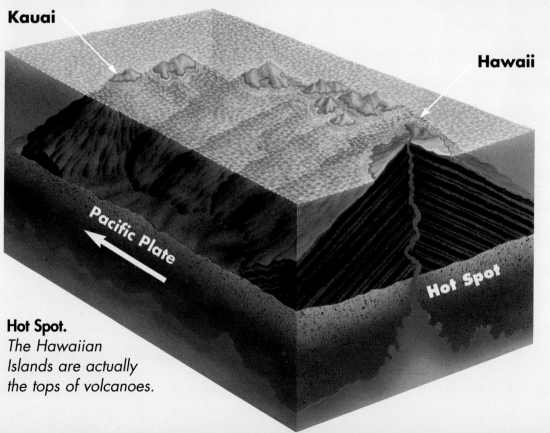

Kauai

Hawaii

Pacific Plate

Hot Spot

**Hot Spot.**
*The Hawaiian Islands are actually the tops of volcanoes.*

Emperor
penguins

**Raising kids in the coldest place on Earth is a tough job. But emperor penguins warm up to the challenge.**

# Penguin Parents

By Sharon Katz Cooper

Have you ever thought about the things your parents or other adult family members do for you? They buy you clothes. They cook you dinner. They help you with your homework. They stand outside in the freezing cold with you for two months to keep you warm. Well, they probably never do that for you. But that's what emperor penguins do so their chicks can survive the winters of Antarctica. This may sound like a royal pain, but for emperor penguins, it goes with the icy territory.

## Family Matters

Every March, temperatures get colder in the Southern Hemisphere. It is autumn, and winter is approaching. Sea ice begins to form around the Antarctic continent. At this time of year, emperor penguins leave the ocean. They waddle across miles of sea ice, heading for the coast. There they gather in breeding areas called **rookeries,** where they find mates and start families.

After a few weeks, the female lays one egg. Then she leaves! Don't worry—she'll come back in about two months. Laying an egg is hard work, so she needs food. She may have to travel 50 miles or more to reach the edge of the sea ice. There she can dive into the ocean for fish.

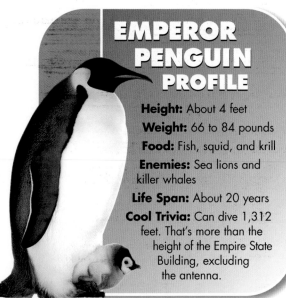

## EMPEROR PENGUIN PROFILE

**Height:** About 4 feet

**Weight:** 66 to 84 pounds

**Food:** Fish, squid, and krill

**Enemies:** Sea lions and killer whales

**Life Span:** About 20 years

**Cool Trivia:** Can dive 1,312 feet. That's more than the height of the Empire State Building, excluding the antenna.

FRANS LANTING/MINDEN PICTURES

## Penguin Pop-sicle

Meanwhile, back at the rookery, it's the male's job to **incubate** the egg. That means he must keep the egg warm enough to hatch. This is no easy task in the middle of winter. Temperatures may drop to minus 76°F. Winds can howl at more than 100 miles per hour. To protect the egg from the icy ground, the male perches it on his feet. Then he covers the egg with his **brood pouch.** This is a flap of skin between his legs. It's covered with feathers except for a bare patch of skin. The egg stays very warm against the bare patch. Inside this "nest," the temperature can be as cozy as 96°F.

Now comes the fun part. Because the male must keep the egg on his feet, he can't move around much. During the next 65 days or so, he shuffles around the rookery with the egg, waiting for the female to return. When blizzards blast him with icy winds and snow, he huddles closely with other emperor dads for warmth. It's dark nearly all the time in Antarctica in the winter. With no food nearby, the penguin papa eats nothing. He survives on the body fat he stored during the summer, when he was gobbling fish, squid, and krill (small, shrimp-like creatures). He'll lose almost half his weight while he keeps his egg warm.

A penguin papa protects the egg for two months. That's how long it takes the mother to head to the ocean, feast on fish, and return to the rookery.

## Trading Places

The female returns about the time the egg hatches. If she is late, or if the egg hatches early, a male emperor can produce a food from his throat. It looks like cottage cheese. The male emperor can feed the chick with his homemade meal for up to two weeks, even though he hasn't eaten in months.

Then it is mom's turn to babysit while dad makes the long trek in search of food. To feed the chick, the female **regurgitates,** or brings back up, seafood she ate on her travels. During the next few weeks, the newborn stays snuggled under her warm pouch. If the chick falls out for even two minutes, it could freeze to death.

## Growing Up

Soon the male comes back, and the parents take turns babysitting and waddling off to find food. When the chick is about seven weeks old, it grows a thick, gray coat of warm feathers. Fuzzy, gray youngsters huddle together in **crèches.** Crèches are a little like day-care centers. While the parents search for food, a few adults stay behind to watch the chicks.

As they grow, young emperors lose their gray feathers and develop black-and-white coats. By this time they are ready to fend for themselves. Antarctica is getting warmer. The sea ice near the rookery starts to break up. That helps young penguins reach the ocean. On their own now, the youngsters dive into adulthood.

## A Breed Apart

Only emperor penguins spend the winter on Antarctica. Every other penguin **species,** or type, heads north to warmer areas. Because of the cold weather, emperors don't mind huddling together tightly to stay warm. No other penguins like to be this close, except with family.

Emperors also raise their chicks a little differently from other penguins. Most species lay two or three eggs at a time, not just one. They usually build nests instead of carrying their eggs. Other penguins also take turns incubating their eggs. Each parent leaves for just a few days at a time to find food. And finally, emperors are the only penguins that hatch their young in the extreme cold of winter.

## WORDwise

**brood pouch:** flap of skin between a penguin's legs

**crèche:** nursery for young penguins

**incubate:** keep an egg warm so it will hatch

**regurgitate:** bring food back up

**rookery:** breeding place for birds or small mammals

**species:** type of plant or animal

# Concept Check

**1** How have sneakers changed since they were first invented?

**2** Why do so many volcanoes form along the Ring of Fire?

**3** How is magma different from lava?

**4** How are penguins able to live and raise young in the coldest place on Earth?

**5** Write something new you learned and one connection that you made.